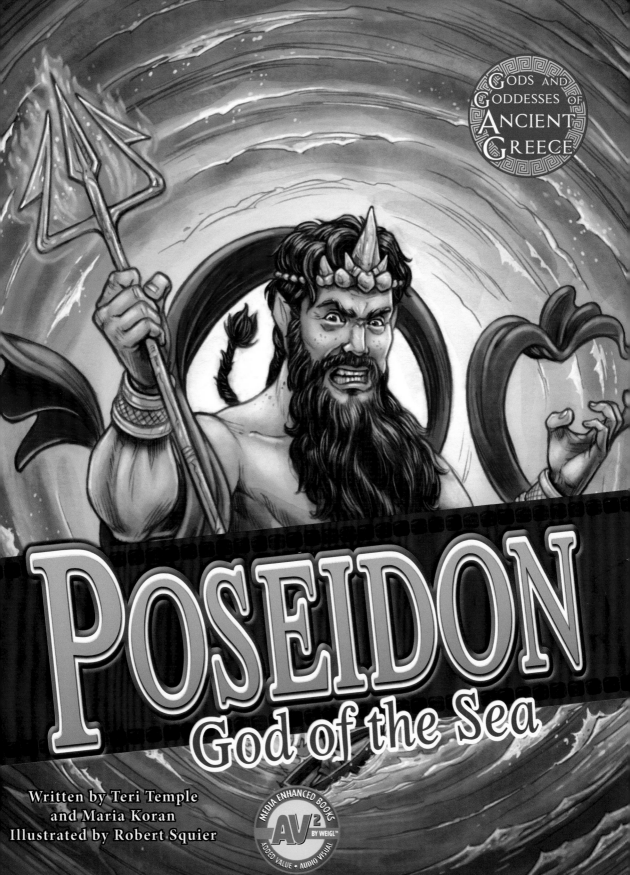

POSEIDON
God of the Sea

Written by Teri Temple
and Maria Koran
Illustrated by Robert Squier

MEDIA ENHANCED BOOKS
AV2 BY WEIGL™
ADDED VALUE • AUDIO VISUAL

www.av2books.com

AV² provides enriched content that supplements and complements this book. Weigl's AV² books strive to create inspired learning and engage young minds in a total learning experience.

Your AV² Media Enhanced books come alive with...

Audio
Listen to sections of the book read aloud.

Key Words
Study vocabulary, and complete a matching word activity.

Video
Watch informative video clips.

Quizzes
Test your knowledge.

Embedded Weblinks
Gain additional information for research.

Slide Show
View images and captions, and prepare a presentation.

Go to **www.av2books.com**, and enter this book's unique code.

BOOK CODE

N933899

AV² **by Weigl** brings you media enhanced books that support active learning.

Try This!
Complete activities and hands-on experiments.

... and much, much more!

Published by AV² by Weigl
350 5th Avenue, 59th Floor
New York, NY 10118
Website: www.av2books.com

Library of Congress Cataloging-in-Publication Data

Names: Temple, Teri, author.
Title: Poseidon / Teri Temple.
Description: New York : AV² by Weigl, 2016. | Series: Gods and goddesses of ancient Greece | Includes index.
Identifiers: LCCN 2016002890 (print) | LCCN 2016004276 (ebook) | ISBN 9781489646514 (hard cover : alk. paper) | ISBN 9781489650467 (soft cover : alk. paper) | ISBN 9781489646521 (Multi-User eBook)
Subjects: LCSH: Poseidon (Greek deity)--Juvenile literature. | Mythology, Greek--Juvenile literature. | Gods, Greek--Juvenile literature.
Classification: LCC BL820.N5 T46 2016 (print) | LCC BL820. N5 (ebook) | DDC 292.2/113--dc23
LC record available at http://lccn.loc.gov/2016002890

Printed in Brainerd, Minnesota, United States
1 2 3 4 5 6 7 8 9 0 20 19 18 17 16

072016
070416

Project Coordinator: Warren Rylands
Art Director: Terry Paulhus

CONTENTS

POSEIDON

INTRODUCTION

Long ago in **ancient Greece** and Rome, most people believed that gods and goddesses ruled their world. Storytellers shared the adventures of these gods to help explain all the mysteries in life. The gods were immortal, meaning they lived forever. Their stories were full of love and tragedy, fearsome monsters, brave heroes, and struggles for power. The storytellers wove aspects of Greek customs and beliefs into the tales. Some stories told of the creation of the world and the origins of the gods. Others helped explain natural events such as earthquakes and storms. People believed the tales, which over time became myths.

The ancient Greeks and Romans **worshiped** the gods by building temples and statues in their honor. They felt the gods would protect and guide them. People passed down the myths through the generations by word of mouth. Later, famous poets such as Homer and Hesiod wrote them down. Today, these myths give us a unique look at what life was like in ancient Greece more than 2,000 years ago.

ANCIENT GREEK SOCIETIES

In ancient Greece, cities, towns, and their surrounding farmlands were called city-states. These city-states each had their own governments. They made their own laws. The individual city-states were very independent. They never joined to become one whole nation. They did, however, share a common language, religion, and culture.

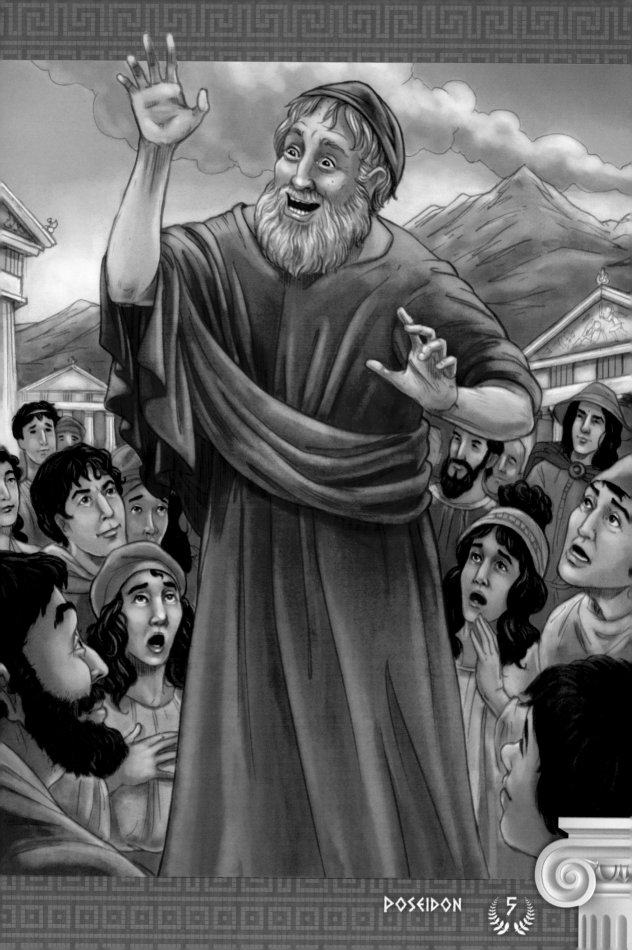

CHARACTERS AND PLACES

Mount Olympus
The mountaintop home of the 12 Olympic gods

Aegean Sea

Athens, Greece
The capital of Greece; patron city of Athena

ANCIENT GREECE

CRETE

Olympian Gods
Demeter, Hermes, Hephaestus, Aphrodite, Ares, Hera, Zeus, Poseidon, Athena, Apollo, Artemis, and Dionysus

Titans (TIE-tinz)
The 12 children of Gaea and Cronus; god-like giants that are said to represent the forces of nature

Trojan War
War between the ancient Greeks and Trojans

Cyclopes (SIGH-clopes)
One-eyed giants; children of Gaea and Uranus

Demeter (di-MEE-tur)
Goddess of the harvest; mother of Persephone

Gaea (JEE-uh)
Mother Earth and one of the first elements born to Chaos; mother of the Titans, Cyclopes, and Hecatoncheires

Medusa (muh-DOO-suh)
A snake-haired creature whose gaze can turn people to stone; mother of Pegasus; killed by Perseus

Minotaur (min-UH-tawr)
Monster on the island of Crete with the body of a man and the head of a bull

Odysseus (oh-DIS-ee-uhs)
Greek hero featured in the epic poems the Iliad and the Odyssey

Orion (oh-RY-uhn)
A handsome giant killed by Artemis; son of Poseidon

Orpheus (OHR-fee-uhs)
Human who traveled to the underworld to rescue his wife Eurydice

Pegasus (PEG-uh-suhs)
A winged horse that sprang from the neck of the beheaded Medusa

Perseus (PUR-see-uhs)
Greek hero who killed Medusa; married to Andromeda

Polyphemus (pah-luh-FEE-muhs)
Man-eating giant blinded by Odysseus; son of Poseidon

Poseidon (puh-SY-duhn)
God of the sea and earthquakes; brother to Zeus

Rhea (RAY-uh)
A Titaness; married to her brother Cronus; mother to the first six Olympic gods: Zeus, Poseidon, Hades, Demeter, Hestia, and Hera

Theseus (THEE-see-uhs)
Greek hero who killed the Minotaur

Aloadae (al-oh-EY-dee)
Twin giants Otus and Ephialtes; sons of Poseidon

Zeus (ZOOS)
Supreme ruler of the heavens and weather and of the gods who lived on Mount Olympus; youngest son of Cronus and Rhea; married to Hera; father of many gods and heroes

Amphitrite (am-fi-TRAHY-tee)
Sea nymph; wife of Poseidon

Athena (a-THEE-na)
Goddess of wisdom; daughter of Zeus

Cronus (CROW-nus)
A Titan who ruled the world; married to Rhea and their children became the first six Olympic gods

THE GOD OF THE SEA

Poseidon was the mighty god of the sea. He was as powerful as the storms he created. Yet he always seemed less powerful than his brother Zeus. Even at the time of their birth, it was Zeus who saved the day.

Their parents were the mighty Titans Cronus and Rhea. Together they gave birth to the first gods. Shortly after their marriage, Cronus learned of a prophecy. A prophecy is a prediction of what is to come.

The prophecy was that one of his children would one day overthrow his rule. This worried Cronus because he had done the same thing to his own father. So Cronus came up with a plan.

As each of his children was born, he swallowed them up whole. This way they would never have a chance to challenge him. His plan seemed to work beautifully. However, it made Rhea sad and lonely. So she came up with her own plan. When the sixth baby was about to be born, Rhea hid the baby on an island. She then gave Cronus a stone wrapped in a blanket. He thought it was the baby and swallowed it up. The baby, safe on the island, grew up to be Zeus. Once he was grown, he decided to rescue his brothers and sisters.

Zeus had the help of his wife Metis. She thought of a way to trick Cronus. Metis gave Cronus a potion to drink. She told him it would make him even mightier. Instead, the potion made him throw up. First he threw up the stone. Then he threw up his children, each in one piece! Poseidon was finally free, along with his siblings Hera, Demeter, Hestia, and Hades. Now they had to deal with their father.

Again Zeus led the way. He led his brothers and sisters in battle against the giant Titans. The battle lasted ten long years. Finally Gaea, or Mother Earth, came to their aid. She told Zeus to free her children, the Cyclopes and the Hecatoncheires, from Tartarus. This place was a prison in part of the underworld. The Cyclopes were mighty one-eyed giants. The Hecatoncheires were monsters. Each had 100 arms and 50 heads. These giants and monsters helped turn the tide of the battle.

The Cyclopes were talented **blacksmiths**. They created special weapons for the three brothers. Zeus got his famous thunderbolts. Hades was given a helmet of invisibility. Poseidon was given his trident. This three-pronged spear could shake the universe.

Finally Poseidon was able to show his great strength. The three brothers decided to work together to defeat the Titans and gain control of the universe. Their father Cronus was destined to share the same fate as his own father.

The ancient Greeks built the Temple of Poseidon high on a cliff at Cape Sounion during the fifth century BC.

The brothers made their final stand. Poseidon used his trident to create a diversion. And the invisible Hades stole all of the Titans' weapons. Then Zeus hit the Titans with his thunderbolts. The crushing blow came as the Cyclopes and the Hecatoncheires battered them with boulders. The fight was finally over.

With peace settling over the lands, a new supreme leader needed to be chosen. Poseidon hoped it would be him. The brothers decided to draw lots to see who would be the king of the gods. To draw lots is to pick an object that represents a choice. When you pick, your decision is based on **chance**. Zeus had the good fortune to draw the best lot. Zeus was to become the new ruler of the universe and king of the gods. Hades would rule the underworld. Poseidon was made god of the sea.

They made their new home on the top of Mount Olympus. There, in a beautiful palace, the gods watched over Earth.

THE REBELLION

Mount Olympus was not always paradise. Shortly after Zeus gained control, the other gods tried to challenge him. Lead by Hera, Poseidon, and young Apollo, they tied Zeus to his bed while he slept. Furious, Zeus threatened to destroy them. But the giant Briareus freed Zeus. For his role in the plot, Poseidon was forced to serve the king of **Troy** for one year.

Poseidon also had a palace under the sea. It was made of **coral** and beautiful gems. He lived there with the sea nymphs, or Nereid, and minor sea gods. Poseidon was known for being moody. On good days, he would calm the seas and create new lands. But when Poseidon was in a bad mood, he would strike the earth with his trident. This caused earthquakes and shipwrecks. All of the seamen of Greece were sure to remember to honor Poseidon. They prayed to him for a safe voyage. If they forgot, he might cause storms and giant waves. Or he could call upon monsters from the deep sea.

Ruling the seas kept Poseidon busy, but he wanted more. He wanted a queen to rule by his side. One day the sea nymphs were dancing and singing on an island. Poseidon noticed the lead singer. She was a beautiful Nereid named Amphitrite. He immediately fell in love. She was not so easy to win though.

BOATING AND SAILING

Boating and sailing were very important parts of ancient Greek life. The people needed a way to buy and sell goods. Sea travel was the easiest way for them to visit other countries to trade. The two main types of ships used in ancient times were military ships and cargo ships.

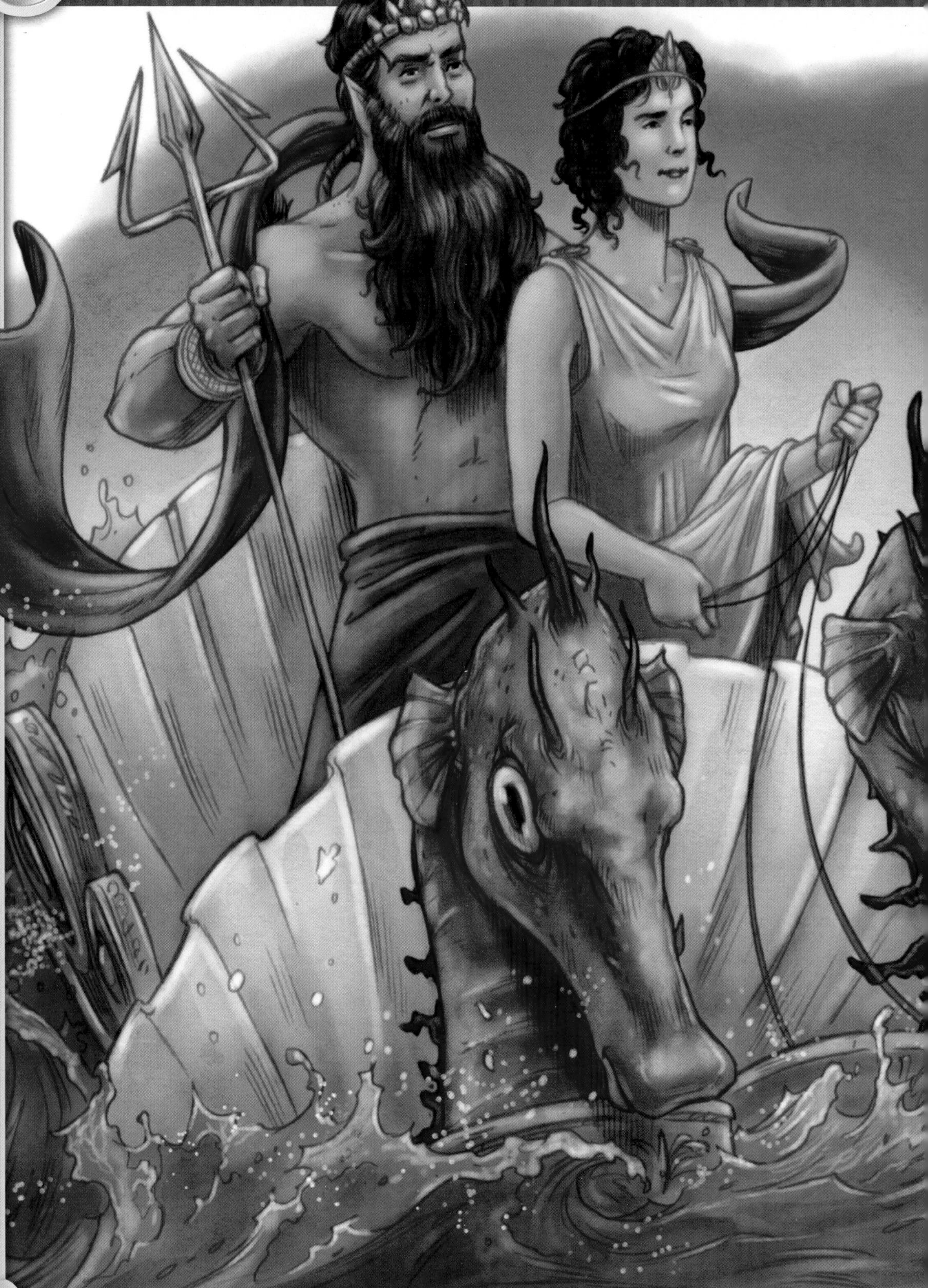

Amphitrite fled from Poseidon to be with the god Atlas. But Poseidon was determined to make Amphitrite his wife. So he sent Delphin, a dolphin god, to fetch her. Delphin convinced Amphitrite to return. She had three children with Poseidon. The most famous was their son Triton. He was Poseidon's messenger. Triton also had godlike powers and could calm the sea at will.

Like his brother Zeus, Poseidon had many wives and children. Amphitrite was not jealous though. She could often be found riding in Poseidon's chariot, which was drawn by sea horses. Amphitrite was content to live in the underwater palace with her sisters.

Some of Poseidon's other famous children were the Aloadae giants, Otus and Ephialtes. They tried to take over Mount Olympus but failed. There was also Charybdis, a monstrous giant chained to the bottom of the sea. She created enormous **whirlpools**. Lastly there was Orion, the handsome hunter. He fell in love with the goddess Artemis.

ORION CONSTELLATION

Orion and Artemis became fast friends. They liked to hunt together in Crete. Stories tell that Artemis accidentally killed Orion while out hunting. He was placed in the stars as a brilliant constellation. Orion's **constellation** is easy to find by the row of three stars that make up his belt. A faint row of stars makes up his sword.

Poseidon had many more well-known children, but he played only a small role in their lives. He chose instead to let them find their own way.

The Minotaur was a monster with the body of a man and the head of a bull. Poseidon had given Minos, the king of Crete, a beautiful bull as a gift. Instead of offering it as a sacrifice, the king chose to keep the bull. Poseidon punished them by causing the king's wife to fall in love with the bull. The king's wife then gave birth to the Minotaur. The Minotaur terrorized the people of Crete. Minos came up with a plan to deal with this problem. He built a labyrinth to contain the monster. A labyrinth is a complex maze. It caused anyone who entered it to become trapped. It became the Minotaur's home. The Minotaur would kill and eat anything it found wandering in the maze.

Minos found a way to keep the Minotaur happy. He waged war against **Athens**. The Athenians knew they were doomed. Their only hope was to send a sacrifice to Minos of seven men and seven maidens. One of those men was Poseidon's son Theseus. Different legends say that Theseus was the son of Aegues, the king of Athens.

Theseus agreed to travel to Crete to destroy the Minotaur and save Athens. When he arrived, he met Ariadne. She was the daughter of Minos. She instantly fell in love with Theseus and told him the secret of the maze. Theseus was able to kill the Minotaur and return home a hero without any help from Poseidon.

Poseidon had another son named Polyphemus. He was a monstrous man-eating Cyclops, one of the Cyclopes. He lived on an island where he **tended** a flock of sheep. The hero Odysseus traveled to this island during his journey home from the Trojan War. He and his men discovered a cave on the island full of food. It was the home of Polyphemus. When he discovered the men, Polyphemus trapped them by blocking the entrance with a large boulder. Polyphemus planned to eat them in the morning.

Odysseus was clever, though, and he thought of an escape plan. Odysseus was ready when Polyphemus returned to the cave that night with his sheep. He gave the Cyclops enough wine to drink so that he fell asleep. Then as he slept Odysseus drove a stake into his one eye. Polyphemus was furious. But he had to let his sheep out to graze. Polyphemus feared that the men would take advantage of his blindness. So he blocked the door and felt each sheep as it left. Odysseus and his men were able to sneak out by tying themselves under the sheeps' bellies.

In his rage, Polyphemus begged his father Poseidon to prevent Odysseus from ever getting home. Poseidon honored his son's request and caused problems for Odysseus for ten long years.

THE TROJAN WAR

Poseidon spent a year building a wall around the city of Troy. This was part of his punishment for trying to take Zeus's rule of Mount Olympus. Poseidon became angry when the Trojan king refused to pay him for his work. Poseidon sent a sea monster to attack Troy as revenge. He sided with the Greeks during the Trojan War, even though Zeus told him to stay out of it. Poseidon made life miserable for everyone during the war.

Poseidon was a restless god. He rarely stayed at home in his palace under the sea. He could often be found racing about in his chariot. He loved all the creatures of the sea, especially his hippocamps. They were creatures that were part horse and part sea serpent. They pulled Poseidon's chariot. Many sea creatures were also his children. Another well-known child of Poseidon's was the beautiful winged horse **Pegasus**.

Poseidon was once in love with the Medusa. She was an attendant to the goddess Athena. When Athena found out, she turned Medusa into a hideous monster. With writhing snakes instead of hair, Medusa was able to turn men to stone with her gaze.

The Greek hero Perseus, a son of Zeus, was sent on a mission to retrieve the head of Medusa. When Medusa was beheaded, the winged horse Pegasus sprung from her neck. It was the child of Medusa and Poseidon. The wild and beautiful horse would go on to play a role in many of Poseidon's stories.

THE HORSE

Ancient Greeks credit Poseidon with creating the horse. Poseidon fell in love with the goddess Demeter. So she issued him a challenge. Demeter asked Poseidon to create the most beautiful animal to walk the earth. He spent many days trying to come up with the perfect animal. His mistakes included the zebra, hippopotamus, and camel. When Poseidon finally made the horse, Demeter was amazed.

Poseidon's temper would often flair when he had to deal with other gods. He was a bit of a bully. When he felt slighted, even Zeus had trouble controlling Poseidon's vicious nature. One place to feel his wrath was the country of Ethiopia.

On his way home from killing Medusa, Perseus saw a beautiful maiden chained to the rocks in the kingdom of Ethiopia. He immediately fell in love. The maiden was the princess Andromeda. Her parents were the king and queen of Ethiopia. Her mother Cassiopeia dared to compare Andromeda's beauty to that of Poseidon's sea nymphs. The sea nymphs pleaded with Poseidon to punish her.

In anger, Poseidon sent the horrible sea monster Cetus to destroy their country. Ethiopia's only hope was Andromeda. She was to be sacrificed to the monster. Perseus struck just as Cetus rose from the waves to devour Andromeda. Able to fly with winged sandals, Perseus killed the sea monster with his sword. Together Perseus and Andromeda lived happily ever after.

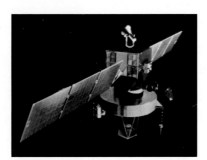

A NASA satellite named after Poseidon was used to help scientists learn about the patterns of ocean circulation.

Zeus was not the only god who frustrated Poseidon. He was often at odds with his niece Athena, the goddess of wisdom. One famous fight involved the city of Athens. Both gods wanted to become the patron of the city. A patron is a protector of a place. The king of Athens was named Cecrops. He was part man and part snake. He thought the best way to decide was to hold a contest. The patron would be the god who created the best gift for the citizens of the city.

Poseidon chose to go first. He wanted to prove his worth. He took his trident and struck the earth with it. Poseidon was so powerful that water burst forth from the ground. The people knew how important water was to their survival. But Poseidon was the god of the sea, so the water was salty. The king did not think too highly of his gift. Next up was Athena.

Athena used her spear to create a hole in the ground. She knelt next to it and planted an olive branch in the space. An olive tree grew from the branch. The ancient Greeks could now harvest the olives for food. The people were very impressed with Athena's gift. Cecrops decided that Athena's gift was more useful to his citizens. So he declared Athena the winner and the patron goddess of his city. Poor Poseidon was left angry and discouraged.

POSEIDON 27

Despite Poseidon's moody nature, many city-states in ancient Greece honored him. Sailors and sea travelers paid respect to him. They offered him sacrifices in hopes that he would grant them calm seas and safe passage. The ancient Greeks also believed he provided them with fresh water and good crops. He was a god best kept happy. They knew at any moment he could strike back in revenge with his powerful storms and damaging earthquakes. Even the Romans adopted Poseidon into their myths. To them he was known as Neptune, the god of the sea.

Poseidon was most often shown as a muscular, bearded, grim god in ancient Greek sculpture. Poseidon is usually seen holding his powerful trident with dolphins at his side. With his great strength and fearsome powers, Poseidon played an important role in the ancient Greek myths.

ISTHMIAN GAMES

The Isthmian Games were a competition that was founded in ancient Greece in 581 BC. They were part of a religious festival to honor Poseidon. It was a chance for the city-states of Greece to come together and celebrate peacefully. The competition was held every other year on the **Isthmus of Corinth**. Men and boys could compete.

The games included boat and chariot races, footraces, boxing, and wrestling. Palm boughs and wreaths of celery leaves were the prizes for the winners.

POSEIDON 29

PRINCIPAL GODS OF GREEK MYTHOLOGY– A FAMILY TREE

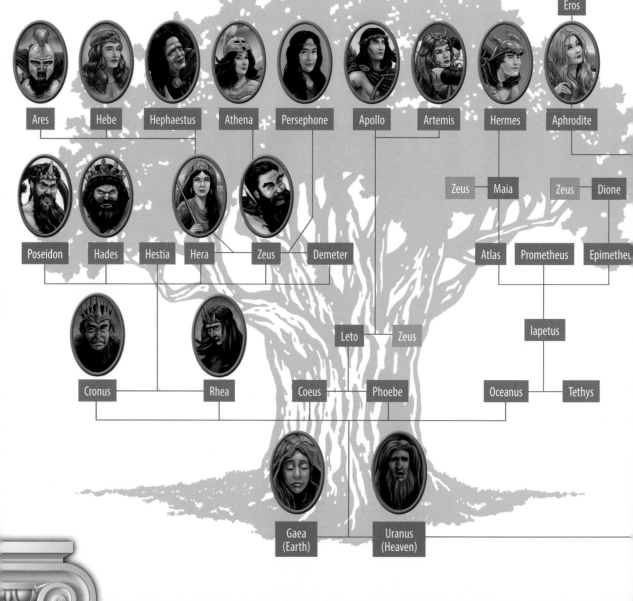

Eros

Ares · Hebe · Hephaestus · Athena · Persephone · Apollo · Artemis · Hermes · Aphrodite

Zeus · Maia · Zeus · Dione

Poseidon · Hades · Hestia · Hera · Zeus · Demeter · Atlas · Prometheus · Epimetheu

Iapetus

Cronus · Rhea · Leto · Zeus · Oceanus

Coeus · Phoebe · Tethys

Gaea (Earth) · Uranus (Heaven)

KEY WORDS

ancient Greece: historical period that lasted from about 800 to 323 BC, during which many advancements were made in politics, art, philosophy, and science

Athens: a busy and beautiful city in ancient Greece that is credited as the birthplace of democracy. Today, Athens is the largest city in Greece and is the country's capital

blacksmiths: people who make or repair items made of iron

chance: the way events happen when not planned or controlled

constellation: a group of stars that creates a shape in the sky and has been given a name

coral: a hard material that forms at the bottom of the ocean from the skeletons of small sea creatures

Isthmus of Corinth: a narrow area of land that connects the Peloponnese to mainland Greece

tended: to serve or take care of someone

Troy: ancient city, the ruins of which are located in modern-day Turkey

whirlpools: an area of water that moves very quickly in a circle

worshiped: showed respect and honor, often through prayer or other religious acts

INDEX

Log on to www.av2books.com

AV² by Weigl brings you media enhanced books that support active learning. Go to www.av2books.com, and enter the special code found on page 2 of this book. You will gain access to enriched and enhanced content that supplements and complements this book. Content includes video, audio, weblinks, quizzes, a slide show, and activities.

AV² Online Navigation

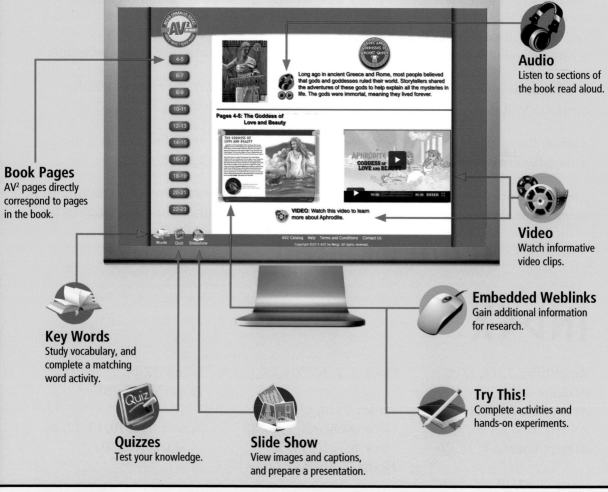

Audio
Listen to sections of the book read aloud.

Book Pages
AV² pages directly correspond to pages in the book.

Video
Watch informative video clips.

Key Words
Study vocabulary, and complete a matching word activity.

Embedded Weblinks
Gain additional information for research.

Quizzes
Test your knowledge.

Slide Show
View images and captions, and prepare a presentation.

Try This!
Complete activities and hands-on experiments.

AV² was built to bridge the gap between print and digital. We encourage you to tell us what you like and what you want to see in the future.

Sign up to be an AV² Ambassador at www.av2books.com/ambassador.